THE
APPLE CIDER VINEGAR
MIRACLE
COOKBOOK

JAKE CARNEY

ALTERNATIVE
DAILY

CONTENTS

INTRODUCTION

I grew up in a very tight knit family. I was very fortunate in that aspect of my life. My parents were always around and we often spent a good amount of time with our grandparents.

If you had a big family or had friends that grew up in big families, you know that almost everything big families do in life revolves around one thing … meals! Even to this day, everything revolves around meals!

One of the first few things my wife and I talk about in the morning is "What's for lunch?" and then, of course, "What do you want to do for dinner?" We're constantly reading new recipes, sharing ideas and planning the next sumptuous spread.

And so the traditions of my family continue with own young daughters, spending time around the table and with family.

Since we have kids of our own now and early bedtime is a must for them, a regimented schedule of meals makes it easier on everyone. I've started companies, hired employees, created great products and grown entire businesses from scratch — yet meal planning and execution is an entirely different ballgame.

So many different deadlines and processes, day in and day out, all to get a hot meal on the table that everyone will enjoy. Shopping, prep work, cooking, grilling, boiling and chopping, serving and clearing, taking care to get each part of each meal just right and a little bit better each time.

It helps that I LOVE to cook.

I love everything about cooking. Shopping for the freshest fruits, vegetables and meats is an exciting part of my day. The variety of interesting things you can do with the same simple set of ingredients is nearly infinite.

Prepping the food, which most people find a drudge, is nearly a form of meditation for me. I love everything about it. Utensils, cutlery, bowls, dishes, cast-irons, stainless, strainers, you name it. For me, it's incredibly fun to play with my cooking "toys" before each meal.

Once you get into cooking you'll find different parts of it to love. Right now, for me, it's all about Japanese knives. The incredible craftsmanship of these miniature swords is second to none. They possess a unique balance of beauty and flexibility and their sharpness is unrivaled.

Then it's game on. All of the hard work and repetition leads up to the moment you start actually using heat — be it a stove, oven, grill, a crockpot, or even cold acidic juices — to cook your food.

Placing a piece of lamb on a hot cast-iron skillet to sear it. Slow-cooking ribs on a grill outside. Using an heirloom dutch oven to reduce a mash of vegetables and beef to a tender masterpiece of spice, fat and flavors. Nothing beats the feeling of putting all your hard work on the line!

Plating the dishes can be an absolute blast. It's the time in your life where you can really be that gourmet chef and make an unbelievable presentation for your family and friends.

I have to admit I usually cook for 8 or more at my house, so it's usually buffet style! But you can make the buffet look like any fancy Manhattan eatery if you try!

APPLE CIDER VINEGAR 101

So what exactly is this stuff you're being told to drink every day?

Here's a quick breakdown so you understand exactly what Apple Cider Vinegar is, and exactly WHY you need to ONLY buy a certain type when you go shopping.

If you take crushed apples and expose them to yeast (either by inoculation, or wild yeast which naturally lives in the environment), the sugars will get fermented, and the result will be alcohol. That's apple cider!

But ACV takes the process one step further. When bacteria gets added into the mix, the alcohol becomes acetic acid. That's the stuff that makes vinegar taste so eye-wateringly sharp. Voila, Apple Cider Vinegar!

Now that you know how Apple Cider Vinegar is produced from alcohol, you'll understand why the word 'vinegar' comes from the French 'vin aigre', meaning sour wine!

Any alcoholic drink left to ferment for too long will become vinegar. Sometimes this is a bad thing (like when you forget to finish that bottle of your favorite Merlot before it goes funky), but it can also be a happy coincidence! That's because the resulting liquid contains powerful proteins, enzymes and beneficial bacteria which make raw vinegars a powerful natural remedy. Plus, it delivers all the nutritional benefits (and more), but contains much less sugar than apple cider or apple juice, with just 3-5 calories per tablespoon.

Traditionally, vinegars are used 'whole' without further processing, leaving the beneficial substances intact. However, In commercial vinegar manufacturing, they are often pasteurized and filtered, which results in a completely different product. One is super healthy, one not so much! We will go further into this in a bit so you know EXACTLY how to choose the BEST vinegar.

But first, let me share with you the fascinating story of Apple Cider Vinegar.

A BRIEF HISTORY OF APPLE CIDER VINEGAR

Did you know that apples weren't originally made for eating?

Until recent decades, apples were too bitter to pick off the tree and munch. They've since been developed into the sweet snack we now know and love. But our ancestors would have only known apples as being useful for one thing: cider!

When water wasn't safe to drink, beer was usually the staple beverage. But in areas where grains were difficult to grow, apples became a favorite for making a fermented drink that was safe to consume on a regular basis.

And what happened when apple cider was left to sit too long? It turned into vinegar! That's how the wonder of ACV was discovered. It's thought that people stumbled upon the phenomenon of vinegar spontaneously, in different parts of the world, around 8000 years ago. And we know that apple trees were growing along the banks of the Nile River by 1300 BC. By 400 BC, Hippocrates, known as the father of modern medicine, wrote about the uses of natural vinegars for good health and medicinal uses. This truly is an ancient and time-tested remedy!

Apple cider spread from the British Isles through the Roman Empire from 55 BC onward, becoming popular across Europe. And since apples grew easily in the New World, colonists in the Americas had a love for cider too. And with that came the love for its sister product, Apple Cider Vinegar.

Although the popularity of alcohol apple cider took a major hit in the prohibition, Apple Cider Vinegar remained a much-loved remedy, and by the 1950s there were popular books in America touting the many healing uses of ACV.

Traditionally, people have used Apple Cider Vinegar in the home for many reasons including cleansing the lymph nodes and liver, as an antiseptic, and to help cure coughs and colds.

MODERN SCIENCE PROVES THE BENEFITS OF APPLE CIDER VINEGAR

Although it's interesting to learn about the historic uses of ACV, what matters today is its track record in scientific studies. Does this ancient remedy stand up to modern science, and is it worth using in 21st century life?

It turns out that there have been a number of studies done on Apple Cider Vinegar, and the results vouch for its healing powers for a number of common health issues and conditions.

Apple Cider Vinegar For Blood Sugar

One of the best-known benefits of Apple Cider Vinegar is to help balance blood sugar. It can improve metabolism, increase insulin sensitivity, and relieve symptoms of diabetes.

Studies have shown that people with metabolic derangement or insulin resistance, and even those with type 2 diabetes, can improve blood sugar balance by 34 percent by drinking Apple Cider Vinegar before meals. This theory started with lab animals such as rats, but has since been tested successfully on humans as well.

Apple Cider Vinegar For Heart Health

If you're worried about the health of your arteries, incorporating more ACV into your diet could be a smart move. Studies show that it can lower LDL, the type of cholesterol that is responsible for clogging arteries, while raising HDL, the "healthy" cholesterol.

Amazingly, Apple Cider Vinegar has also been shown to keep blood pressure levels healthy. Scientists have found that ACV consumption inhibits an enzyme which would normally raise blood pressure. This makes it a solid preventative remedy for maintaining a strong heart and circulatory system.

Weight Loss With Apple Cider Vinegar

Thousands of people around the world have shared stories about successful weight loss using Apple Cider Vinegar. And science backs this up.

When Apple Cider Vinegar enters your mouth, the sharp taste stimulates the production of saliva and enzymes. It also fires up the production of digestive compounds in the stomach and intestines, meaning that food is digested more efficiently, helping clear out and detox the system better as well. That means healthier toilet habits!

As a result your metabolism is boosted and you get more nutrients (and higher energy levels) from eating less food! It's no surprise that weight loss is an effortless result with all these positive effects.

Digestive Benefits of Apple Cider Vinegar

Many people mistakenly believe that poor digestion is due to too much acid in the digestive system, so they take antacids and the like. In reality, low acid levels are more commonly the culprit behind discomforts like heartburn and acid reflux.

That's why Apple Cider Vinegar is such a helpful remedy for better digestion. Not only does it have acetic acid which can relieve symptoms of acid reflux, but it also introduces helpful enzymes and probiotic bacteria which support good metabolism and detox.

Apple Cider Vinegar For Beauty

Not only can ACV make you healthier but it can also make you more beautiful!

Many people swear by Apple Cider Vinegar as a toner for a clearer complexion, helping to tighten pores, cleanse skin and even lighten age spots.

Consuming ACV can also make you more beautiful from the inside out, since improved digestion and detox helps create a glowing youthful skin tone, fresher breath, and a brighter, whiter look to the eyes.

Other beauty benefits of Apple Cider Vinegar include keeping nails healthy, supporting a healthy scalp and making hair shiny and manageable.

Now that you know all the ways ACV can change your life, aren't you excited to get your hands on a bottle? Next we will reveal the do's and don'ts of shopping for Apple Cider Vinegar.

HOW TO BUY THE BEST APPLE CIDER VINEGAR

Apple Cider Vinegar can be a powerful remedy for health and beauty. However, it only works if you buy the right type.

If you check out the shelves at your grocery store or health shop, you'll see various types of bottles labelled "Apple Cider Vinegar", but they're not all the same. The most common types are translucent and even in color, without any visible particles floating inside. This is a sure sign that the vinegar has been pasteurized and filtered to create a mainstream commercial product. Many people believe this processing removes much of the vinegar's medicinal power.

The one you're looking for is unpasteurised, raw, unfiltered Apple Cider Vinegar. Even better if it's organic. You'll be able to tell a good brand because the vinegar will be cloudy, with visible pulp and stringy bits floating in it. These are the living cultures that give ACV it's probiotic benefits.

If you're looking at a bottle of Apple Cider Vinegar at the grocery store, and you're not sure, here's the bottom line: If it doesn't specifically say "raw" on the label, it's probably been pasteurized, and you're best to keep looking.

What To Look For On Your ACV Label

Make sure your Apple Cider Vinegar label features the following key words:

- Raw
- Unpasteurised
- Unfiltered
- Organic
- With "The Mother"
- Probiotic
- Unprocessed
- Living cultures

As long as you buy the right type of Apple Cider Vinegar, you'll be able to enjoy all the health benefits from integrating this ingredient into your lifestyle.

So now you know how to shop for the best ACV, but do you know what to do with it?

HOW TO USE APPLE CIDER VINEGAR FOR YOUR HEALTHY LIFESTYLE

Many people stick to the basic way to use Apple Cider Vinegar, but it's actually a highly versatile ingredient.

The most common starting point is to simply mix a small amount of Apple Cider Vinegar into a glass of water, and drink it in the morning. Some people also prefer to have a glass before every meal to boost digestion.

It's important to note that Apple Cider Vinegar should never be consumed straight. Do not drink it from the bottle, or take it with a spoon. The acetic acid may damage your dental enamel, or the tissues in your mouth and throat. It's safer to dilute the vinegar in at least half a glass of water.

Most experts recommend an amount ranging from 1 teaspoon, to 2 tablespoons. If you don't like the taste of the basic water and ACV mixture, never fear, we have many delicious drink ideas coming up in the recipe section!

Popular ACV recipes include smoothies, salad dressings and marinades. It also makes a flavorful addition to soups and roast dishes. There are even desserts that incorporate Apple Cider Vinegar!

Besides food and drink, here are some more ways to put that bottle of ACV to good use:

- Kill weeds in the garden: Spray ACV directly on to weeds
- Detoxing bath soak: Put a cup in the bath to tone and cleanse skin, and reduce harmful bacteria, yeast and fungus
- Antibacterial mouthwash: Dilute and rinse the mouth daily for fresh breath
- Hair rinse: Mix with water and splash over hair for a dandruff-free scalp and shiny, manageable hair
- Vegetable rinse: Remove residues from produce by rinsing in a bowl of water with a tablespoon of ACV added
- Sore throat remedy: Gargle with diluted ACV, or mix with honey and consume like a cough syrup
- Natural household cleaner: Mix with water in a spray bottle and use as an antibacterial cleaner
- Treat skin conditions: Apply diluted ACV to toenail fungus, poison ivy rash, athlete's foot or warts
- Flea treatment: Use half-and-half water with ACV in a spray bottle to treat pets

Now that you're well acquainted with the wonders of Apple Cider Vinegar, you must be raring to go and get started! You'll be surprised how many ways you can work this important dietary supplement into your cuisine, whether they are old favorites, or new and exciting things to try.

Without further ado, let's get into some recipes! Enjoy!

RECIPES

CATEGORIES

Drinks & Remedies

Dressings & Marinades

Soups, Salads & Sides

Protein Dishes

Desserts & Snacks

Apple Cider Vinegar
Morning Metabolism Booster

SERVING SIZE:	8 Ounces
MAKES:	1 Serving
COOK TIME:	2 Minutes

Keto-friendly option
Gluten-free
Vegan

Try starting your day with this energizing and detoxing drink that will boost your digestion and fire up weight loss.

INGREDIENTS

8 oz warm water

1 Tbsp apple cider vinegar

1 Tbsp fresh lemon juice

1 tsp ground cinnamon

1 tsp honey (omit for keto)

INSTRUCTIONS

1 Start with some warm water in your favorite mug.

2 Add apple cider vinegar, lemon juice, cinnamon and honey, and mix well.

3 Enjoy your drink while it's warm.

Chia and ACV Digestive Elixir

SERVING SIZE: 1 Cup
MAKES: 1 Serving
COOK TIME: 5 Minutes

Keto-friendly
Gluten-free
Vegan

Drink this simple beverage regularly to get glowing skin and a strong metabolism, plus relieve digestion and ease heartburn.

INGREDIENTS

1 Tbsp whole chia seeds

Juice of ½ lemon

1 Tbsp apple cider vinegar

1 ½ cups warm water

INSTRUCTIONS

1 Mix all the ingredients together in a glass.

2 Let rest for 5 minutes, stirring occasionally, or until the chia seeds have formed a gel. Drink up!

Keto "Kombucha" Fizz

SERVING SIZE: 1 Glass
MAKES: 1 Serving
COOK TIME: 5 Minutes

Keto-friendly
Gluten-free
Vegan

This refreshing drink will kick any cravings for soda and even makes a great mocktail. The probiotic-rich ACV stands in for kombucha as a low-carb alternative. Get creative with different combinations of low-sugar fruits, like berries or citrus, and add herbs such as mint, basil or rosemary for a flavor kick.

INGREDIENTS

2 tsp apple cider vinegar

1 cup sparkling mineral water, or soda water

1 thin slice of apple, diced

2 thin slices of ginger root

INSTRUCTIONS

1   Start with a few ice cubes in a glass.

2   Add the diced apple, ginger slices, and apple cider vinegar, then top up the glass with sparkling water.

3   Mix gently, and enjoy!

ACV-na Colada Tropical Detox Drink

SERVING SIZE:	1 Tall glass
MAKES:	1 Servings
COOK TIME:	5 Minutes

Keto-friendly
Gluten-free

This exotic fruity drink seems more like an island cocktail than a healthy remedy! It's deliciously packed with nutrient-rich ingredients that will nourish and energize your body.

INGREDIENTS

1 Tbsp ginger

3 lemons

3 Tbsp apple cider vinegar

**1 Tbsp raw honey or maple syrup
(Manuka honey if possible,
or sub 2-3 drops stevia for keto)**

1 cup coconut water

**1 small starfruit
(sliced, optional for garnish)**

INSTRUCTIONS

1   Grate the ginger root.

2   Halve and juice the lemons.

3   Mix all ingredients in a tall glass, swirl and enjoy.

4   Optionally enjoy over ice on a hot day.

ACV-Spiked Green Smoothie

SERVING SIZE:	Tall glass
MAKES:	1 Serving
COOK TIME:	10 Minutes

Keto-friendly
Gluten-free
Vegan
Plant-powered

A nourishing green smoothie complete with Omega 3s and Probiotics to kick off your morning or power up your afternoon.

INGREDIENTS

1 ½ oz baby spinach

1 green zucchini

1 apple, chopped

1 tsp cinnamon

1 Tbsp apple cider vinegar

3 Tbsp walnuts

1 cup water

1 cup ice cubes

INSTRUCTIONS

1   Chop the apple and zucchini.

2   Measure all ingredients into a blender or NutriBullet.

3   Whiz until smooth, and enjoy!

Fiery ACV Cold Remedy

SERVING SIZE:	Shot glass
MAKE	1 Pint
COOK TIME:	Prep time 10 minutes
	Plus 3-6 weeks brew time

Gluten-free
Plant-powered

A simple and effective remedy traditionally used to relieve sinus congestion, ward off colds and flus, aid digestion, and increase circulation.

INGREDIENTS

½ cup peeled and
diced horseradish

½ cup peeled and diced garlic

½ cup peeled and diced onion

¼ cup peeled and diced ginger

¼ cup peeled and diced turmeric

1 habanero chile, split in half

1 orange, quartered and
thinly sliced crosswise

½ lemon, quartered and
thinly sliced crosswise

½ cup chopped parsley

2 Tbsp chopped rosemary

2 Tbsp chopped thyme

1 tsp black peppercorns

2 to 3 cups raw unfiltered apple
cider vinegar (at least 5% acidity)

¼ cup raw honey,
or more to taste

INSTRUCTIONS

1 Place all of the vegetables, fruits, herbs, and spices in a large clean jar. Fill the jar with vinegar, covering all the ingredients and making sure there are no air bubbles. Cap the jar. If using a metal lid, place a piece of parchment or wax paper between the jar and the lid to prevent corrosion from the vinegar. Shake well.

2 Let the jar sit for 3 to 6 weeks, shaking daily (or as often as you remember).

3 Strain the vinegar into a clean jar. Add honey to taste. Refrigerate and use within a year. Can be used as a cold remedy or for flavoring sauces, dressings, soups and drink mixes.

Keto Apple Cider Vinegar Salad Dressing

SERVING SIZE: 1-2 Tablespoons
MAKES: 2 Servings
COOK TIME: 5 Minutes

Keto-friendly
Gluten-free
Vegan

Avoid all the sugars, vegetable oils and additives in conventional salad dressings, and make your own! This simple recipe ticks all the boxes. Try it on top of a high protein shrimp salad with lots of colorful vegetables.

INGREDIENTS

2 oz extra virgin olive oil

2 oz apple cider vinegar

**1 Tbsp erythritol
(or use honey for non-keto)**

2 garlic cloves

1 tbsp mustard

Dried herb blend

Salt and pepper to taste

Instructions

1 Finely chop the garlic cloves.

2 Whisk together olive oil, apple cider vinegar, and sweetener in a bowl.

3 Add garlic, mustard, herb blend and seasonings, and mix well.

4 Store in a jar so you can shake up the salad dressing before use.

Tangy Green Goddess Dressing

SERVING SIZE:	3-4 Tablespoons
MAKES:	6 Servings
COOK TIME:	15 Minutes

Keto-friendly
Gluten-free
Vegan
Plant-powered

Enjoy this nutrient-rich dressing with a kale salad, drizzle over roasted vegetables, or use as a dip for chicken.

INGREDIENTS

1 garlic clove

1 ½ medium avocados

¼ cup extra virgin olive oil

⅓ cup water

¾ cup basil leaves

¼ cup chopped parsley

¼ cup chopped chives

½ cup chopped scallions

Juice of 1 medium lemon

2 Tbsp apple cider vinegar

1 tsp salt

INSTRUCTIONS

1   In a food processor or high-speed blender, blend together garlic, avocado, olive oil, water, basil, parsley, chives, scallions, lemon juice, apple cider vinegar, and salt until smooth and creamy.

2   Serve over your favorite dishes.

3   Store in a jar or sealed container in the fridge for up to 3 days.

Apple Cider Vinegar Marinade

SERVING SIZE:	1 Tablespoon
MAKES:	3 Servings
COOK TIME:	5 Minutes

Keto-friendly
Gluten-free
Vegan

This simple marinade adds delicious flavor to steak, chicken, pork or grilled vegetables.

INGREDIENTS

1 Tbsp apple cider vinegar

1 Tbsp avocado oil (or MCT oil)

1 garlic clove

1 Tbsp dijon mustard

Salt and pepper to taste

INSTRUCTIONS

1 Finely chop the garlic clove.

2 Mix all ingredients together in a small bowl, combining well with a whisk.

3 Place meat or veggies in a large dish, pour marinade overtop and cover the dish. Allow to sit for a minimum of 30 minutes, or overnight in the fridge.

ACV Probiotic Hummus

SERVING SIZE:	2 Tablespoons
MAKES:	8 Servings
COOK TIME:	10 Minutes

Gluten-Free
Vegan
Plant-powered

Hummus is great for a healthy snack, or addition to your favorite meals. Keep a jar in the fridge for easy access to nourishing ACV anytime.

INGREDIENTS

¼ cup olive oil

15 oz canned chickpeas (rinsed)

3 garlic clove

2 Tbsp tahini

3 Tbsp lemon juice

2 tsp cumin

1 Tbsp apple cider vinegar

Pinch of salt

½ tsp paprika

2 Tbsp water

INSTRUCTIONS

1 Measure all of the ingredients into a blender.

2 Blend everything together, adding a little more water if needed.

3 When your hummus is smooth, break out the carrots, pita chips or pretzels and enjoy.

Vegan Nacho Dip

SERVING SIZE:	3-4 Tablespoons
MAKES:	6-8 Servings
COOK TIME:	20 Minutes

Gluten-free
Vegan
Plant-powered

Enjoy this spicy "cheese" dip with nacho chips or a Mexican-inspired salad. It's packed with nutritious ingredients, so, vegan or not, everyone should give it a try!

INGREDIENTS

2 Tbsp olive oil

½ large yellow onion, finely diced

3 cloves garlic, minced

2 large carrots, very finely chopped

1 cup thinly sliced butternut squash

2 tsp kosher salt, divided

1 tsp ground cumin

½ tsp chili powder

¼ tsp freshly ground black pepper

1 cup low-sodium vegetable broth

1 (4-ounce) can green chiles, drained

1 ½ cups unsweetened plain almond milk

1 cup raw cashews, soaked for 30 minutes or up to overnight and then drained

¼ cup nutritional yeast

½ cup chunky tomato salsa or pico de gallo

1 Tbsp apple cider vinegar

OPTIONAL TOPPINGS:

Chunky salsa

Pickled jalapeños

Chopped cherry tomatoes

Fresh Chopped Cilantro

INSTRUCTIONS

1   Heat the olive oil in a large saucepan over medium heat until shimmering. Add the onions and garlic and sauté until the onions are soft and the garlic is fragrant.

2   Add the carrots, butternut squash, 1 teaspoon of the salt, cumin, chili powder, and black pepper. Cook, stirring occasionally, for a couple of minutes. Add the vegetable broth and simmer, stirring frequently, until the vegetables are soft and tender. You want them to be soft enough to blend up in a blender without any problems.

3   Transfer the mixture to a high-powered blender. Add the green chiles, almond milk, drained cashews, nutritional yeast, salsa, vinegar, and remaining 1 teaspoon salt. Blend, scraping down the sides as needed, until the mixture has reached a thick and creamy consistency.

4   Taste and adjust the seasoning as needed. If it's cooled off, transfer to a saucepan and gently warm over low heat to desired temperature. Serve it in a bowl alongside tortilla chips and garnish it with your favorite toppings. Leftovers can be stored in an airtight container in the refrigerator for up to 5 days.

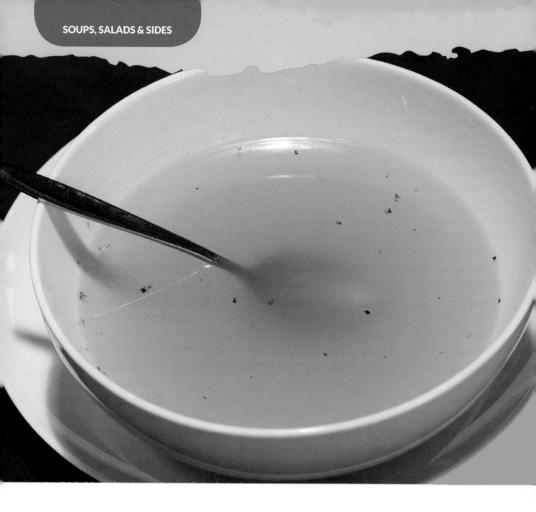

Apple Cider Vinegar Bone Broth

SERVING SIZE:	1 Cup
MAKES:	10 Servings
COOK TIME:	8 to 24 hours

Keto-friendly
Gluten-free

Make your own gelatin-rich bone broth to keep skin hair and nails healthy, lubricate joints and heal the gut lining. Store bones in the freezer until you have enough to make a batch of broth.

INGREDIENTS

2 Tbsp apple cider vinegar

Soup bones, or leftover bones from roast dinners - enough to fill your slow cooker

Water

INSTRUCTIONS

1   Fill up your crock pot or slow cooker with bones.

2   Cover the bones with water.

3   Add 2 tablespoons of apple cider vinegar.

4   Turn the slow cooker on High for 2-3 hours, then turn it down to low for the rest of the cook time. Cook for at least 8 hours, preferably 24 or more.

5   Check the slow cooker periodically to see if it needs more water. The water should always be covering the bones.

6   Once your broth is ready, remove the bones with tongs, and ladle the broth into jars or containers for storage. The broth can be frozen if you won't be using it quickly.

Cozy & Nourishing Lentil Soup

SERVING SIZE:	1 ½ Cups
MAKES:	4 Servings
COOK TIME:	1 Hour 15 Minutes

Gluten-free
Vegan
Plant-powered

This nutrient-packed soup will warm you up and leave you feeling full for hours afterward. A great dish for a cold day or to pack along for lunch.

INGREDIENTS

½ Tbsp coconut oil

1 cup chopped onion

½ Tbsp minced garlic

1 Tbsp apple cider vinegar +
½ Tbsp extra

1 tsp basil

1 bay leaf

4 cups low sodium
vegetable stock

1 tsp miso

1 can whole peeled tomatoes

½ head green cabbage

½ teaspoon sriracha

1 ⅓ cup green lentils

Ground pepper + sea salt,
to taste

INSTRUCTIONS

1 Place the lentils in a bowl of water and soak overnight. Or, if you want to make the soup today, use canned lentils (rinse well before using).

2 In a large soup pot, heat coconut oil over medium heat. Add onions, cook and stir until onion is tender. Stir in garlic, bay leaf and basil; cook for 2 minutes. Add 1 Tablespoon of apple cider vinegar to deglaze the pot.

3 Add stock, canned tomatoes, cabbage, miso and sriracha. If you're using soaked lentils, add them now as well (if using canned lentils, add in the next step). Bring to a boil, then reduce heat, and simmer for at least 30 minutes.

4 If you're using canned or pre-cooked lentils add them now, then continue to simmer the soup for 20 more minutes.

5 Season to taste with salt, pepper and additional apple cider vinegar before serving.

Herby Halloumi Bruschetta

SERVING SIZE:	1-2 Slices
MAKES:	3-4 Servings
COOK TIME:	15 Minutes

Gluten-free option
Plant-powered

For an easy and delicious way to enjoy the probiotic power of ACV, put together this bruschetta recipe for a quick snack or appetizer.

INGREDIENTS

**Fresh baguette
(or use gluten-free)**

7 oz halloumi cheese

2 Tbsp apple cider vinegar

1 Tbsp honey

4 roma tomatoes

Handful fresh basil leaves

Freshly ground salt and pepper

INSTRUCTIONS

1 Start with a warm, fresh baguette and cut it into slices.

2 Broil the slices for two minutes, cover them, and set them aside.

3 Next, in a slightly warm frying pan, heat up the halloumi cheese cut into quarter-inch slices. Cook the cheese until both sides are golden brown, and then set them aside as well.

4 Heat up the apple cider vinegar and honey in a saucepan for five minutes on medium heat, stirring the entire time.

5 Put the bread slices on a serving dish, top with the cheese, and drizzle the ACV and honey mixture on top.

6 Finally, add a slice of Roma tomato and a basil leaf to each piece of bread, and sprinkle salt and pepper on the whole scrumptious ensemble!

Crunchy & Colorful Summer Salad

SERVING SIZE: 1 Cup
MAKES: 4 Servings
COOK TIME: 20 Minutes

Gluten-free
Vegan
Plant-powered

A medley of bright and healthy vegetables dressed up with a punchy ACV-based dressing. Enjoy as a delicious accompaniment next to your favorite protein dish.

INGREDIENTS

FOR THE DRESSING:

1 ½ Tbsp apple cider vinegar

3 Tbsp extra virgin olive oil

2 tsp dijon mustard

1 tsp raw honey

½ tsp sea salt

½ tsp ground coriander

Freshly ground black pepper, to taste

FOR THE SHAVED SALAD:

4 small golden beets, peeled

4 medium carrots, peeled

1 small bunch of radishes, trimmed & cleaned

2 Tbsp chopped flat-leaf parsley

INSTRUCTIONS

1 Whisk the dressing ingredients together in a large bowl.

2 Thinly slice the beets, carrots, and radishes on a mandolin or in a food processor with the slicing disc.

3 Toss the sliced vegetables with the dressing to coat evenly.

4 Sprinkle with chopped parsley, season to taste with additional salt and freshly ground pepper if desired, and serve.

Honey Roasted ACV Carrots

SERVING SIZE:	½ Cup
MAKES:	8 Servings
COOK TIME:	15 Minutes Prep
	40 Minutes Cooking

Gluten-free
Plant-powered

These sweet and savory carrots make a great side dish for any meal. Use the leftovers cold on top of salads.

INGREDIENTS

**3 Lbs carrots,
peeled and sliced on an angle**

3 Tbsp olive oil

**Salt and freshly ground
black pepper**

3 Tbsp honey

1 ½ Tbsp apple cider vinegar

2 ½ Tbsp chopped fresh parsley

1 Tbsp fresh thyme leaves

INSTRUCTIONS

1 Preheat oven to 400 degrees.

2 Place carrots on a 17 by 12-inch rimmed baking sheet. Drizzle with olive oil and season with salt and pepper and toss to evenly coat. Spread into an even layer.

3 Roast in preheated oven 20 minutes then remove from oven.

4 In a small bowl stir together honey and apple cider vinegar. Drizzle carrots with honey mixture and toss well to evenly coat. Return to oven and roast about 10 to 20 minutes longer.

5 Remove from oven, toss again and sprinkle with fresh parsley and thyme. Serve warm.

Rainbow Salad With Mint and Cumin ACV Vinaigrette

SERVING SIZE: 1 Cup
MAKES: 6 Servings
COOK TIME: 15 Minutes

Gluten-free
Vegan
Plant-powered

You'll love this bright salad as a fresh and tasty side dish to lighten up your meal. Makes a great alternative to coleslaw.

INGREDIENTS

**1 cup uncooked quinoa
(any color), rinsed and drained**

2 cups water

2 large oranges

¼ cup extra virgin olive oil

2 tsp apple cider vinegar

½ tsp honey or agave nectar

**½ tsp coriander seeds,
toasted and lightly crushed**

1/2 tsp salt

freshly ground black pepper

¼ cup chopped cilantro

**1 ½ cups (or 1 can) cooked
black beans, rinsed and drained**

½ small red onion, thinly sliced

INSTRUCTIONS

1. Place quinoa and water in a small saucepan. Bring to a boil, cover, and simmer over low heat. Simmer for about 15 minutes, or until all liquid is absorbed. Remove from heat and let stand for 5 minutes. Fluff quinoa with a fork and spread on a parchment-lined baking sheet to cool.

2. Prepare oranges while quinoa is cooling. Finely grate the zest of one orange and set aside. Segment both oranges, reserving the juice (squeeze the orange membranes after segmenting), and set aside.

3. In a small bowl, whisk together orange zest, 3 tablespoons of orange juice, olive oil, apple cider vinegar, honey, coriander seeds, salt, a few cracks of pepper, and chopped cilantro. Adjust seasonings if desired.

4. Place quinoa, black beans, onion, and orange segments in a large bowl and stir gently to combine. Pour dressing over salad and toss gently to coat.

5. Serve immediately or refrigerate until ready to serve. Optionally garnish with feta or halloumi cheese for delicious flavor.

Low Carb Noodle Bowl
With ACV Dressing

SERVING SIZE:	1 ½ Cups
MAKES:	2 Servings
COOK TIME:	20 Minutes

Keto-friendly
Gluten-free
Vegan
Plant-powered

Zucchini noodles tossed with fresh greens and an apple cider vinegar dressing makes a healthy lunch or side dish.

INGREDIENTS

FOR THE ONIONS:

1 large red onion, thinly sliced

1 Tbsp ghee

salt and pepper

FOR THE SALAD:

2 medium-large zucchini

1 cup cherry tomatoes, halved

½ yellow bell pepper, diced

packed ½ cup arugula

minced basil for garnish

FOR THE DRESSING:

3 Tbsp olive oil

2 Tbsp apple cider vinegar

1 tsp dijon mustard

½ tsp italian seasoning

Salt and pepper

INSTRUCTIONS

1 Heat up a pan over medium heat and melt the ghee (or any cooking oil you prefer). Toss in the thinly sliced onions, season with a dash of salt and pepper and stir.

2 Turn down the heat to medium-low and let the onions cook while you prepare the salad. Keep an eye on the onions and stir occasionally so that they cook evenly. After about 10 minutes, you can remove them from the heat and set the pan aside to cool.

3 Make noodles with your zucchini with your spiralizer (the blade with the smallest triangles) or you can use a vegetable peeler instead to make thin zucchini ribbons.

4 Place the zoodles in a large bowl and toss in the tomatoes, pepper and arugula.

5 In a small bowl, whisk together the dressing ingredients.

6 Measure 1 cup of the cooked onion and add to the salad.

7 Pour the dressing over the vegetables and toss it all to combine. Garnish with fresh basil and serve.

8 Optionally, add some chopped pepperoni or salami for an Italian-style lunch bowl.

Creamy Quinoa Chopped Lunch Bowl

SERVING SIZE: 1 ½ Cups
MAKES: 2 Servings
COOK TIME: 15 Minutes

Gluten-free
Vegan
Plant-powered

This crunchy and creamy quinoa salad makes a great lunch with heaps of vitamins and fiber, plus the probiotic punch of Apple Cider Vinegar.

INGREDIENTS

1 cup diced sweet potatoes

2 cups chopped romaine

1 cup shredded brussels sprouts

1 cup chickpeas

½ cup quinoa

½ cup chopped pecans

FOR THE DRESSING:

3 Tbsp tahini

1/4 cup apple cider

1 Tbsp apple cider vinegar

1 Tbsp lemon juice

1-2 tsp fresh sage finely chopped

½ tsp sea salt

½ tsp red pepper flakes

fresh pepper if desired

INSTRUCTIONS

1. Steam the sweet potatoes for about 10 minutes until tender. Rinse under cool water and allow to cool completely.

2. To shred the brussels sprouts, use a knife to slice them very thinly, or use a box grater on the largest setting, a mandolin slicer or a food processor.

3. In a large mixing bowl, combine romaine, brussels sprouts, chickpeas, quinoa, pecans and cooled sweet potatoes. Set aside.

4. In a small bowl, whisk together the dressing ingredients. Taste and adjust seasoning with fresh pepper if desired.

5. Pour dressing over salad and toss to combine.

6. Serve salad immediately (or chill for no more than 20 minutes). Garnish with additional chives and chili flakes if desired.

7. Optionally, add grilled chicken or salmon for more protein.

Pineapple Turmeric Sauerkraut

SERVING SIZE:	¼ Cup
MAKES:	20 Servings
COOK TIME:	45 Minutes to prep,
	4-7 Days to ferment

Keto-friendly
Gluten-free
Vegan
Plant-powered

Packed with enzymes, probiotics and fiber, this homemade sauerkraut is a must-have for a healthy gut.

INGREDIENTS

1 head of cabbage, shredded

½ pineapple, chopped

1 Tbsp ground turmeric

1 Tbsp fresh ginger, grated

1 Tbsp sea salt

FOR THE BRINE:

1 Tbsp sea salt

1 Tbsp raw apple cider vinegar

4 cups purified water

INSTRUCTIONS

1 Shred the cabbage in a food processor, mandolin or chop with a knife. Put it in a large mixing bowl.

2 Chop the pineapple into small chunks and add it to the bowl with the cabbage.

3 Add in grated ginger and sea salt.

4 Massage the cabbage mixture with your hands for 5 minutes or until it starts to break down and become soft.

5 Let it sit for 15 minutes in the bowl.

6 After 15 minutes, the cabbage will become very soft and wet. If you squeeze it now, juice will come out.

7 Add the turmeric to the cabbage and mix with a spoon.

8 Pack the cabbage halfway into a large mason jar.

9 Make the brine by combining 1 cup of hot water with the sea salt. Once the sea salt dissolves, add the remaining water and the apple cider vinegar.

10 Pour the brine into the mason jars, leaving about an inch from the top. Stir the brine and cabbage together in the jar so it's all combined.

11 Place a lid on the jar loosely so gas can escape as fermentation takes place. Set on the counter for 4-7 days in a cool, shaded place. Put a dish under the sauerkraut in case the juices bubble over. During fermentation the sauerkraut will bubble a little and become cloudy. If scum appears, remove it with a spoon.

12 Every day or two, shake the mason jar up so the cabbage submerges under the brine and doesn't develop mold.

13 After the fermentation period, place in the fridge and serve cold.

14 Enjoy the extra brine from the sauerkraut as a probiotic 'gut shot' - simply serve in a shot glass and drink.

Dill Pickled String Beans

SERVING SIZE:	3-4 Beans
MAKES:	6 Servings
COOK TIME:	15 Minutes prep time
	Plus 24 hours pickling time

Keto-friendly
Gluten-free
Vegan
Plant-powered

These dill pickled beans are an excellent source of vitamin K, manganese, vitamin C, dietary fibre, folate, and vitamin B2, plus the probiotics from ACV! Use the beans as a salad topper or an addictive snack.

INGREDIENTS

1.5 cups green beans (washed and trimmed)

½ cup fresh dill (chopped)

1 garlic clove

1 tsp red pepper flakes (optional)

1 tsp black peppercorns

1 cup apple cider vinegar

½ cup water

1 tsp sea salt

INSTRUCTIONS

1 Trim the ends from the green beans and cut them into equal lengths that will fit into a 500 mL mason jar.

2 Place the dill, garlic, red pepper flakes and peppercorns into the bottom of the jar. Turn the jar on its side and tightly pack the beans in. Set jar aside.

3 In a medium sauce pan combine apple cider vinegar with water and sea salt. Bring to a boil. Once boiling, reduce to a simmer. Let simmer for 3 minutes.

4 Pour the vinegar into the jar with the beans. Cover with a lid and let cool. Transfer to the fridge and let sit for at least 24 hours before eating. Flavour will intensify over time. Enjoy as a snack, side dish, or chopped on top of salads.

Sticky Sweet Brined Ribs

SERVING SIZE:	Half rack of ribs
MAKES:	4 - 6 Servings
COOK TIME:	4 Hours

Gluten-free option

These mouth-watering ribs will convert even the most determined ACV-haters. The vinegar tenderizes the meat and the succulent sauce is a flavor sensation everyone will love. Be sure to buy extra servings because everyone will want seconds!

INGREDIENTS

BRINE:

1 cup apple cider vinegar

4 cups water

2 Tbsp sea salt

2 Tbsp cracked black pepper

10 garlic cloves

3 lbs baby back ribs, in half-racks

Half bottle of beer or cider
(use cider for gluten free)

1 onion, quartered

BARBECUE SAUCE:

1 Tbsp olive oil

1/2 cup chopped onion

1 Tbsp minced serrano pepper

1 Tbsp minced garlic

1 Tbsp minced ginger

2 Tbsp apple cider vinegar

2 cups apple sauce

1/2 can of tomatoes

3 Tbsp molasses

INSTRUCTIONS

BARBECUE SAUCE:

1 In a medium saucepan over medium-high heat, add the olive oil, onion and serrano pepper, and cook until the onion is translucent.

2 Stir in the garlic and ginger and cook for 1 to 2 minutes longer, being cautious not to burn the mixture.

3 Pour in the vinegar and mix everything together, allowing to cook briefly, then add the tomatoes, apple sauce and molasses. Stir to combine, then lower heat and simmer for 15 minutes.

4 Puree with an immersion blender, then strain through a sieve into a bowl or jar. If you don't use it all, your remaining sauce can be stored, covered, in the refrigerator for up to a week.

RIBS:

1 Preheat an indoor or outdoor grill to high.

2 Preheat the oven to 400 degrees F.

3 In a large resealable bag, combine the vinegar, water, 1 tablespoon of the salt and 1 tablespoon of the pepper, 4 of the garlic cloves and the ribs. Let sit at room temperature for 15 minutes.

4 Remove the ribs from the brine and season both sides with the remaining salt and pepper. Sear the ribs on the grill until lightly browned.

5 In a large roasting pan, arrange the ribs and pour in half of the beer or cider. Add the onion and remaining garlic cloves. Cover the pan tightly with aluminum foil and put into the hot oven. Reduce the heat to 300 and roast for 1 1/2 hours. Remove the foil and baste the ribs with the BBQ Sauce. Roast for 7 minutes, then turn the ribs over, baste again and roast for another 7 minutes.

6 Remove the ribs from the oven to a cutting board and slice between the ribs. Arrange on a serving platter and serve.

Paleo Shrimp With ACV

SERVING SIZE:	½ Cup of shrimp
MAKES:	6 Servings
COOK TIME:	30 Minutes

Keto-friendly
Gluten-free

This flavorsome shrimp recipe will make you LOVE eating healthy. It is packed with protein and anti-inflammatory ingredients. Serve with salad or a veggie stir fry for a complete meal.

INGREDIENTS

**2.5 lbs shrimp
(deshelled and deveined)**

2 Tbsp brown cumin seeds

2 Tbsp fresh minced garlic

½ cup apple cider vinegar

1 tsp turmeric powder

3 red chilis, minced

1 tsp sea salt

1 Tbsp olive oil

½ Tbsp coriander seeds

INSTRUCTIONS

1 Dry roast the cumin seeds, coriander seeds and garlic together in a non-stick pan until golden. Allow to cool.

2 Use a mortar and pestle, or the back of a large spoon, to grind the roasted spices with apple cider vinegar and red chillies. The result will be a fine paste.

3 In a pan add the olive oil and the paste mix. Mix well, then add the turmeric powder and salt.

4 Cook on medium heat until the oil rises to the surface and the mixture turns orange in color.

5 Turn down the heat and add the shrimp. Mix carefully until all the shrimp are well coated in the spice mixture. Cover the pan with a lid for a couple of minutes to ensure the shrimp cook through. Enjoy with some salad, rice or stir fry.

One-Dish Hearty Roast Dinner

SERVING SIZE: 2 Cups
MAKES: 4 Servings
COOK TIME: 50 Minutes

Keto-friendly option
Gluten-free
Plant-powered

This is the easiest dinner to throw in the oven, with satisfying results, and only one dish to wash afterward! You'll love the rich flavor added by the ACV.

INGREDIENTS

1 ½ lbs chicken breasts

1 lb butternut squash, peeled and cubed

1 (8 oz) package white mushrooms, left whole

4 oz brussels sprouts, halved

3 carrots, peeled and coined

1 yellow onion, chopped

(for keto-friendly option, omit butternut squash, carrot and onion, and add zucchini, cauliflower and asparagus)

FOR THE MARINADE:

½ cup apple cider vinegar

¼ cup olive oil

2 Tbsp honey

2 cloves garlic, pressed

1 tsp dijon

¼ tsp salt

¼ tsp pepper

1 tsp dried thyme

1 tsp dried rosemary

INSTRUCTIONS

1 Whisk together marinade.

2 Place chicken breasts and marinade together in a plastic baggie or tupperware and let marinate in fridge for at least 30 minutes, or overnight.

3 Preheat oven to 425 degrees F and line a baking sheet with a silicone mat or baking paper.

4 Place all prepared vegetables onto baking sheet.

5 Remove the chicken breasts from the fridge and place on a plate. Set aside.

6 Use the marinade from the chicken and pour it over the vegetables. Toss to coat.

7 Bake the vegetables in the oven for 20 minutes, stirring halfway through.

8 Place the chicken onto the baking sheet and bake for an additional 20 minutes, stirring the vegetables halfway through.

9 Chicken should be cooked through and vegetables should be tender.

10 If the vegetables aren't tender, remove the chicken and let rest while you cook the vegetables for an additional 5-10 minutes.

11 Season with more salt if necessary, and serve while it's hot.

Sardine Snacking Toasts

SERVING SIZE: 1-2 Toasts
MAKES: 2 Servings
COOK TIME: 10 Minutes

Gluten-free option

Even if you don't think you like sardines, give this recipe a try. The pickled onions really tone down the fish flavor, and your body will thank you for the nutrient boost.

INGREDIENTS

FOR THE PICKLED ONIONS:

1 small red onion
(about 5 ounces)

½ cup apple cider vinegar

½ cup water

½ tsp granulated sugar

½ tsp fine salt

FOR THE TOASTS:

4 wasa crispbreads (or choose
your favorite gluten-free option)

4 tsp dijon mustard

1 (3.5 ounce) can sardines

INSTRUCTIONS

1 Peel and halve the onion lengthwise. Thinly slice the halves and set aside.

2 Bring the vinegar, water, sugar, and salt to a boil in a medium saucepan over medium-high heat, stirring to dissolve the salt and sugar. Remove from the heat, add the onion, and stir to combine, making sure all the onions are submerged in the liquid. Let sit for 15 minutes before using.

3 Spread a teaspoon of mustard on each crispbread. Lifting the sardines out of their canning liquid with a fork, divide the sardines among the crispbreads and gently smash into an even layer with the back of a fork. Place a thin layer of pickled red onions over the sardines (save the remaining onions for another use) and serve immediately.

Crispy Buttery Shrimp

SERVING SIZE:	½ Cup of shrimp
MAKES:	4 Servings
COOK TIME:	20 Minutes

Gluten-free option

These savory shrimp are delicious on top of gluten free pasta or spiralized vegetables for a protein-rich, plant-powered meal.

INGREDIENTS

¼ cup apple cider vinegar

8 Tbsp butter

2 tsp minced garlic

32 large shrimp, peeled

¼ tsp red pepper flakes

Pinch of creole or
cajun seasoning

½ cup grape tomatoes, halved

½ cup green onion, chopped

2 tsp fresh chopped parsley

2 tbsp breadcrumbs
(or gluten-free breadcrumbs)

salt and pepper to taste

1 Tbsp fresh chopped parsley,
to serve

1 lemon, sliced into wedges

INSTRUCTIONS

1 Heat butter in a large nonstick skillet over medium-high heat. Add garlic and cook for 1 minute.

2 Add shrimp, red pepper flakes, and Creole/Cajun seasoning, and sauté until shrimp turns pink.

3 Toss in grape tomatoes, green onions, and parsley and cook for one minute.

4 Deglaze pan with Apple Cider Vinegar and cook for 2 more minutes.

5 Place on oven-proof serving dishes and sprinkle with breadcrumbs / gluten-free breadcrumbs. Turn oven to broil, and cook for 1 minute or until top is golden brown.

6 Garnish with the additional chopped parsley and lemon wedges.

7 Serve on top of gluten-free pasta, spiralized vegetable 'pasta', or vegetables of your choice.

Creamy Apple Cider Vinegar Chicken

SERVING SIZE:	1-2 Chicken thighs
MAKES:	4 Servings
COOK TIME:	35 Minutes

Keto-friendly
Gluten-free

Try this warming chicken recipe when you need some extra energy or a health boost. It's like a cozy hug in food form.

INGREDIENTS

1-1/3 lbs boneless chicken thighs (about 7 thighs)

1 Tbsp extra-virgin olive oil

Sea salt and black pepper

1 medium onion, sliced

4 large garlic cloves, smashed

⅔ cup raw apple cider vinegar

1 cup chicken broth

5 sprigs fresh thyme

1 can full-fat coconut milk (use the thick cream on top, and keep the thin liquid for another use)

INSTRUCTIONS

1 Heat the oil in a large skillet over medium-high heat.

2 Season the chicken with salt and pepper.

3 Add the chicken to the pan and brown on both sides.

4 Remove the cooked chicken to a plate and add the onions and garlic to the pan. Stir for one minute.

5 Pour in the vinegar and stir, scraping up any browned bits on the bottom of the pan.

6 Pour in the broth. Put the chicken back into the pan and add the thyme sprigs and raw Chinese herbs if using them.

7 Cover and simmer for 20 minutes, or until it's cooked through (flipping the chicken over halfway through).

8 Remove the chicken from the pan and pour the coconut cream into the pan. Whisk until combined well and let simmer about 5 minutes, or until the sauce starts to thicken a bit.

9 Discard the thyme sprigs and serve.

World Famous Pulled Pork

Gluten-free option

Impress your friends and family with this delicious pulled pork recipe with ACV. The time and effort you'll put in is well worth the delicious flavor and texture of the succulent end result.

INGREDIENTS

3-4 lbs pork butt

1 sweet onion

3 cloves of garlic

2 cups yellow mustard

1 ½ cups coconut sugar

1 ½ cups apple cider vinegar, plus extra ½ cup

¼ cup water

½ cup sierra nevada pale ale, plus extra (or beer of your choice) (use hard cider for gluten-free)

4 Tbsp chili powder

2 tsp black pepper

2 tsp white pepper (if you don't have white pepper add 1 more teaspoon of black pepper)

1/2 tsp cayenne pepper

1 tsp soy sauce (use tamari for gluten-free)

4 Tbsp butter

2 Tbsp liquid smoke

INSTRUCTIONS

1 Turn your crock pot on high. Pour a splash of beer or cider, and 1/2 cup ACV into the crock pot.

2 Cut onion into long strips and add into the crock pot. Mince the cloves of garlic and add.

3 Trim fat off pork butt and add into crock pot, then close the lid.

4 Mix all of the above ingredients (except butter) in a large bowl with a mixer. Pour the sauce over the pork butt in the crock pot, then place the butter on top of the pork.

5 Close the lid. If you cook on high, let it cook while turning every few hours for 5 hours. If you cook on low, let it cook for 8 hours while turning every few hours.

6 When the pork appears to be falling apart, take it out and place it on a large cutting board, baking sheet or dish. Use a fork to pull the pork apart. Take fat pieces out. Put the pulled pork back in the crock pot and turn the crock pot to low for half an hour.

7 Serve steaming hot with your favorite side dishes.

Easy Chicken Adobo

SERVING SIZE:	1 Chicken thigh, ½ Cup rice (optional)
MAKES:	4-6 Servings
COOK TIME:	30 Minutes

Keto-friendly option
Gluten-Free option

A flavorful Philippine-inspired recipe with a rich flavorful sauce. Make it in an Instant Pot for a quick and delicious dinner.

INGREDIENTS

2 lbs skin-on, bone-in chicken thighs

⅔ cup apple cider vinegar

⅓ cup tamari or soy sauce (use tamari for gluten-free)

10-12 cloves garlic, peeled and smashed

2 bay leaves

1 tsp coarsely ground black pepper, plus more as needed

Salt

Steamed white rice, for serving (optional, omit for keto)

INSTRUCTIONS

1 Place the chicken thighs, skin-side down, in a 6-quart or larger Instant Pot. Add the vinegar, tamari or soy sauce, garlic, bay leaves, and black pepper.

2 Secure the lid on the Instant Pot, then make sure the valve is in the "Sealing" position. Set the Instant Pot to Pressure Cook on High for 15 minutes. Allow the Instant Pot to release its pressure naturally. Meanwhile, line a rimmed baking sheet with aluminum foil. Arrange a rack in the middle of the oven and heat to broil.

3 Open the Instant Pot. Using tongs, transfer the chicken skin-side up to the baking sheet, and set aside. Press the "Sauté" button on the Instant Pot and set the timer for 10 minutes, stirring occasionally and mashing the garlic in the sauce with a wooden spoon if desired, so that the sauce can reduce. Meanwhile, broil the chicken.

4 Broil the chicken until nicely browned, rotating the baking sheet as needed, 3 to 5 minutes. When the sauce is ready, taste and season with salt and additional pepper as needed. Discard the bay leaves. Serve the chicken thighs with steamed white rice if desired, and ladle the sauce over the chicken and rice.

5 For a keto-friendly option, serve over greens or spiralized veggies.

Chocolate Frosted Cupcakes

SERVING SIZE:	1 Cupcake
MAKES:	12 Servings
COOK TIME:	35 Minutes

Gluten-free
Vegan

You'll love these chocolatey cupcakes which have a surprise healthy ingredient in the frosting! They have about half the calories of a conventional chocolate cupcake, with all the delicious flavor.

INGREDIENTS

FOR THE CUPCAKES:

½ cup almond flour

½ cup white rice flour

½ cup coconut flour

½ cup sugar

¼ cup unsweetened cocoa powder

1 tsp baking soda

½ tsp salt

3 ripe bananas

½ cup apple sauce

¼ cup unsweetened almond milk

1 tsp apple cider vinegar

1 tsp vanilla extract

FOR THE FROSTING:

2 ripe avocados

¼ cup unsweetened cocoa powder

3 Tbsp maple syrup

½ tsp vanilla extract

INSTRUCTIONS

1 Preheat oven to 180°C. Line a muffin tin with 12 paper or silicone cups.

2 Combine flours, sugar, cocoa powder, baking soda, and salt in a medium bowl. Set aside.

3 In a separate medium-sized bowl, mash the bananas with a fork. Add the apple sauce, almond milk, ACV and vanilla extract, and mix well.

4 Slowly add the dry ingredients to the wet to form a smooth batter.

5 Divide the batter evenly between the 12 cupcakes.

6 Bake for 20 to 25 minutes, or until a toothpick inserted comes out clean. Remove from the oven, and after a few minutes, move cupcakes to a cooling rack.

7 While the cupcakes bake, make the icing. Scoop out the avocado flesh, and place in a food processor.

8 Add the cocoa powder, maple syrup, and vanilla, and puree until smooth.

9 Frost the cooled cupcakes, and enjoy!

Iced Lemon Cake

SERVING SIZE:	1 Slice
MAKES:	8-10 Servings
COOK TIME:	50 Minutes

Gluten-free option
Vegan

This delicious dessert has been made over with healthier ingredients, so you can enjoy a citrusy treat guilt-free.

INGREDIENTS

FOR THE LEMON CAKE:

1 cup unsweetened organic soy milk or almond milk

1 tsp apple cider vinegar

1 cup plus 2 tbsp flour (or gluten-free flour)

⅓ cup almond meal

1 ½ tsp baking powder

½ tsp salt

¾ cup coconut sugar

⅓ cup coconut oil (melted)

Juice from half a small lemon (about 1 tablespoon)

2 tsp pure lemon extract

FOR THE LEMON ICING:

½ cup powdered sugar

1 Tbsp unsweetened organic soy milk or almond milk

½ tsp lemon extract

INSTRUCTIONS

1. Preheat oven to 350F. Lightly spray a loaf pan.

2. In a medium bowl, whisk together the milk and apple cider vinegar, and set aside.

3. In a large bowl, mix together the flour, almond meal, baking powder, and salt.

4. In the medium bowl with the milk and vinegar mixture, add the sugar, oil, lemon juice, and lemon extract, and mix well.

5. Make a well in your dry ingredients, pour in the wet, and stir until just combined.

6. Pour batter into the loaf pan, and bake for 35-40 minutes or until a toothpick inserted comes out clean.

7. Let sit for about 10 minutes before removing from the pan to cool on a wire rack.

8. Whisk together the ingredients for the icing. Once the cake is completely cool, drizzle on top and enjoy!

Fresh Fruit Salad Bowl

SERVING SIZE:	1 Cup
MAKES:	3-4 Servings
COOK TIME:	10 Minutes prep
	Plus 1 hour marinating time

Gluten-free
Vegan
Plant-powered

Here's a fresh and surprising take on fruit salad, packed with nutrients which will brighten your skin and make you smile.

INGREDIENTS

¼ cup freshly-squeezed orange juice

1 tsp seasoned rice vinegar

1 tsp granulated sugar

2 cups peeled and diced cucumber

1 cup blueberries

1 cup diced strawberries

1 large fuji apple, cored and chopped

Fresh mint, for serving (optional)

INSTRUCTIONS

1 In a small bowl, combine orange juice, vinegar, and sugar. Stir until blended and set aside.

2 Place cucumber, blueberries, strawberries, and apple in a large bowl. Top with the orange juice mixture and stir gently to coat.

3 Cover and refrigerate for at least 1 hour (overnight is best). Stir gently just before serving. Garnish with mint, if using. Enjoy!

Vegan Dark Chocolate Donuts

SERVING SIZE: 1 Donut
MAKES: 12 Servings
COOK TIME: 20 Minutes

Gluten-free
Vegan

Probably the healthiest chocolate donut on the planet! If you don't have a donut tin, it's well worth buying one to try out this awesome recipe. They're easy to find online or at specialty kitchen stores.

INGREDIENTS

FOR THE DONUTS:

1 cup garbanzo beans (chickpeas), rinsed and drained

½ cup unsweetened almond milk (or soy)

¾ tsp baking powder

¼ tsp baking soda

2 tbsp vanilla extract

1 tsp apple cider vinegar

½ tsp salt

½ cup sugar

¾ cup vegan chocolate chips (such as ghirardelli semisweet chips)

½ cup white rice flour

½ cup almond flour

FOR THE FROSTING:

½ cup vegan chocolate chips

1 Tbsp unsweetened almond milk (or soy)

½ Tbsp vanilla

¼ cup organic powdered sugar

INSTRUCTIONS

1 Preheat oven to 350ºF.

2 Place the garbanzo beans, almond milk, baking powder, baking soda, vanilla, apple cider vinegar, salt, and sugar in a blender or NutriBullet. Blend until smooth.

3 Melt the chocolate chips in the microwave in a large glass mixing bowl. Pour in the pureed mixture and flours, and stir until a thick batter forms.

4 Spray two doughnut pans with cooking spray.

5 Using a small spoon, carefully fill each doughnut well, smoothing out the batter with the back of the spoon.

6 Bake for 8-10 minutes.

7 Allow to cool in the pan for 5 minutes before moving to a cooling rack.

8 While they're cooling, make the frosting. Melt 1/2 cup of chocolate chips in a small bowl. Stir in the almond milk, vanilla, and powdered sugar.

9 Spread onto each doughnut, decorate as you like, and enjoy immediately!

10 Store uneaten doughnuts in an airtight container and enjoy within a day or two.